W9-ACO-715

THE OLYMPICS

CRISES AT THE OLYMPICS

HAYDN MIDDLETON

The Olympic Spirit

The modern Olympic Games began in 1896. Since then the Games' organizers have tried to ensure that every competitor keeps to the true Olympic spirit. This spirit is based on fair play, international friendship, a love of sport purely for its own sake, and the ideal that it is more important to take part than to win.

Heinemann Library
Des Plaines, Illinois

Designed by AMR
Originated by Dot Gradations
Printed in Hong Kong/China

04 03 02 01 00
10 9 8 7 6 5 4 3 2 1

Library of Congress Cataloging-in-Publication Data
Middleton, Haydn.
     Crises at the Olympics / Haydn Middleton.
          p. cm. – (Olympics)
     Summary: Surveys the history of the Olympics and explores some of
     the incidents, controversies, scandals, and tragedies associated
     with the modern Olympic games.
      ISBN 1-57572-452-9 (library binding)
     1. Olympics—History Juvenile literature. [1. Olympics-
     -History.] I. Title. II. Series: Middleton, Haydn. Olympics.
     GV721.53.M53 2000
     796.48'09—dc21   99-22709
                                                        CIP

Acknowledgments
The Publishers would like to thank the following for permission to reproduce photographs:
Allsport, pp. 6, 7, 8, 10, 12, 13, 15, 19, 24, 25, 26, 27, 28, 29; IOC Olympic Museum, p. 4,
Pressens Bild, p. 5; Associated Sports Photography, pp. 17, 20; Colorsport, pp. 16, 18, 21;
Corbis/Bettmann, p. 14; Kobal Collection/Warner Brothers Pictures, p. 11; Popperfoto, p. 22;
Sporting Pictures (UK) Ltd, p. 23.

Cover photograph reproduced with permission of AP File.

Every effort has been made to contact copyright holders of any material reproduced in this
book. Any omissions will be rectified in subsequent printings if notice is given to the Publisher.

Any words appearing in the text in bold, **like this**, are explained
in the Glossary.

Contents

Introduction

The modern Olympic Games began in 1896. With breaks during World Wars I and II, they have been held at four-year intervals ever since. The first Games were staged in Greece, home of the Olympics in ancient times. The next scheduled Games will be held in Sydney, Australia, in the year 2000.

The 1996 organizers called the Games in Atlanta, Georgia, "the largest peacetime social event in human history." It would be hard to argue with that. From small beginnings in 1896, the Games have become a wonderful celebration of international sport and of healthy competition.

Tarnish on the gold

Over the years, however, these peaceful Games have featured a high number of incidents, controversies, scandals, and even tragedies. This book tells about some of those crises. They range from the appalling organization of the 1900 Games in Paris to the outrage caused at Seoul in 1988 when "the Fastest Man on Earth" tested positive for drugs.

Adolf Hitler watches over the opening of the 1936 Olympic Games in Berlin, Germany.

As you will see, many problems have arisen when Olympic sports mixed with politics. Some people say that sports and politics are completely separate and should always stay that way. But as the Games grew bigger, and more and more people took an interest in them through the **media**, governments realized that they could use the Olympics to score political points over their rivals and enemies.

4

No one knew this better than Adolf Hitler, whose **Nazi** Party ruled Germany when the Games were held in Berlin, Germany, in 1936. Hitler planned to turn the Olympics into a showcase for the all-around supremacy of the German people. He attempted to undermine the true Olympic spirit.

Political rivalry at the Games became especially open and bitter after 1952. The United States and the **USSR**, the two global superpowers, seemed to conduct a type of peacetime warfare through their athletes. Their rivalry grew until, in 1980, the United States refused to send a team to the Olympic Games in the USSR. Then in 1984, the USSR stayed away from the Los Angeles Games in California. These unfortunate **boycotts** kept the Games from being a true worldwide event.

Problems in perspective

Perhaps we should not be surprised that there have been so many Olympic crises. Any event that brings together competitors from so many nations (197 nations in Atlanta in 1996) is bound to have problems. The dream of Olympic glory drives men and women from all over the world to great heights of achievement. The same dream has also been behind the stories told here.

Sports and politics clashed violently when terrorists entered the Olympic Village at Munich in 1972.

Is This the Olympic Games?

Today, when the Olympic Games are held, TV, radio, and newspapers make sure that people all over the world know what is happening. But the first three Games of the modern era—Athens in 1896, Paris in 1900, and St. Louis in 1904—were not so well publicized. Plenty of people remained blissfully ignorant that these Games were being staged. In fact, even some competitors were unaware that they were involved in the Olympics. Good organization was not a feature of the modern Games' early history!

Farce in France

Compared to what followed in 1900 and 1904, the 1896 Games in Athens were a miracle of efficiency. The quality of the sport was often low, but the large crowds had a wonderful time. Afterwards, many Greeks thought that the Games should always be held in their country. But Baron de Coubertin, the father of the modern Olympic Movement, had an international vision, and the second Games in 1900 were scheduled to take place in Paris, France, his home country.

This turned out to be a bad idea. That year, a great fair called the Universal Exposition was also being held in Paris. The Games, strung out from May to October, turned out to be little more than a sideshow within the exposition. Spectators were few and far between, facilities and officials were often of a poor standard, and very few people seemed to know what was going on. Margaret Abbott of the United States won the women's golf event. She explained her win by saying that "all the French girls apparently misunderstood the nature of the game scheduled for that day and turned up to play in high heels and tight skirts."

This poster is for the 1900 Games in Paris, which were part of a much larger fair. Facilities for the athletes were poor and public interest was very low.

Jeux Olympiques

PARIS 1900

When the 1900 Games limped to an end, even de Coubertin had to admit that "we have made a hash of our work." He could only hope that the 1904 Olympics, to be held across the Atlantic Ocean in St. Louis, Missouri, would be a big improvement. But maybe he guessed that they would not be successful, because he did not even travel to St. Louis himself, nor did many foreign competitors.

Absurdity in America

The 1904 Games were held as part of the World's Fair. Again, events were spread out over a period of months, rather than days. Again, the level of official incompetence was very high. One eyewitness said, "I was not only present at a sporting contest, but also at a fair where there were sports, where there was cheating, where monsters were exhibited as a joke."

The 1904 Games in St. Louis, Missouri, were the last to be linked to an international fair.

Maybe the lowest point came during the Anthropology Days, when athletic contests ranging from pole climbing to stone throwing were arranged purely for "savage peoples" that included Africans and native North and South Americans. Afterwards, one of the organizers concluded that "the savage has been a very overrated man, from an athletic point of view." Such an insulting and racist attitude toward fellow human beings would not, of course, be tolerated today.

For a while after 1904, public interest was so low that it seemed there would be no more Games at all. Then in 1906 an **interim** Games was held in Athens in an attempt to get back to the spirit and success of 1896. In this, the Games largely succeeded and whetted the world's appetite for the next official Games in London in 1908. But London had its own troubles.

Do You Need Assistance?

The London Games of 1908 were well-organized, but there was plenty of arguing, too. The competitions themselves were organized by the British. This led to protests from the French, Canadians, Italians, and Swedes about official rulings. But the most bitter opposition came from representatives of the United States, especially over the twice-run 400-meter final that ended up being won by the only British runner. Later the International Olympic Committee (IOC) gave the control and judging of individual competitions to the international federation that governed each sport. The story of what happened in the marathon race shows why this was a good idea.

The man with ideal legs

The marathon race took place on July 24—a hot, muggy day. The course began at Windsor Castle and ended at the Olympic stadium in London, 26 miles 385 yards (about 42 kilometers) away. The 385 yards at the end were to be run around the stadium track, so that the finishing line was right in front of the **royal box**.

After 20 miles (32 km) it seemed like a two-man race for the gold. The leader was South African Charles Hefferon, but closing fast was a small, short-legged Italian from Carpi.

Dorando Pietri was illegally helped over the finish line of the marathon race at the 1908 London Olympics.

The Italian's name was Dorando Pietri. When asked if the shortness of his legs was a problem for a marathon runner, he said that they were ideal since they were "exactly long enough to reach from the hips to the ground!"

Everybody loves you when you're down and out

The crowd lining the route now took a big hand in events. Hefferon, tiring, accepted a glass of champagne from someone two miles from the stadium. This was not a good idea. He soon had stomach cramps and grew dizzy. Well-wishers then urged Pietri so enthusiastically that he quickened his pace too far from the finish.

The spectators inside the stadium saw the Italian runner appear first. He had only 385 yards (352 meters) to go. But in his exhaustion he was running the wrong way! The track officials rushed to set him in the right direction, and then he collapsed. What should the officials and doctors do? Should they just leave him there or run to his aid? If they helped, he would be disqualified. They decided to get him back to his feet. As Pietri kept plodding, he kept falling down, and his helpers kept rushing to pick him back up. But now a second runner entered the stadium. Not Hefferon from South Africa, but Bob Hayes from the United States! Jack Andrews, the race's head organizer, saw Hayes coming, then looked and saw Pietri falling yet again, so he caught the Italian and carried him across the line.

The Italian flag was hoisted up the victory pole even as Hayes crossed the line himself. Naturally the Americans made a furious protest. It was upheld, and while Pietri was carried away on a stretcher, Hayes was declared the rightful winner. This avoided an all-out war between the U.S. supporters and the British officials. The next day Pietri, fully recovered, claimed that he would have won without help. Queen Alexandra presented him with a **consolation** gold cup. Although he hadn't won a medal, the story of his run soon made him more famous than many true Olympic champions.

What Is a Professional?

The 1912 Olympics in Stockholm have been called the Harmonious Games. Unlike the previous Games in St. Louis, Paris, and London, they were well-organized and well-reported. They passed without any major problems at the time. But a year later, there was a news story about one of the athletes who had taken part. One of the biggest Olympic controversies was about to be uncovered.

Bright Path's road to fame

Jim Thorpe was born in 1888 to parents of mixed Native American, French, and Irish blood. His mother gave him the Indian name Wa-tho-huck, meaning "Bright Path." Jim first won national fame as a football player. He also won the 1912 **intercollegiate** ballroom dancing championship. In that year, he was chosen as a member of the United States Olympic team. As befitted so versatile an athlete, his events were to be the **track and field pentathlon** (long jump, javelin throw, discus throw, 200-meter run, 1,500-meter run) and the **decathlon** (long jump, javelin throw, discus throw, 1,500-meter run, high jump, pole vault, shot put, 110-meter hurdles, 100-meter run, 400-meter run).

Thorpe won gold medals in both events. He was also presented with a jewel-encrusted cup by the czar of Russia. Then King Gustav V of Sweden gave him a bronze **bust** for winning the pentathlon. "Sir," he said to Thorpe, "you are the greatest athlete in the world." And the shy Thorpe replied, "Thanks, King!" Thorpe returned to the United States and a ticker tape parade in New York City.

Jim Thorpe had never competed in a decathlon before winning the gold medal at the 1912 Olympics. His performance was so good that it would have won him a silver medal years later at the 1948 Games.

10

Jim Thorpe sold the movie rights to his life story in 1931 for $1,500. Twenty years later, a movie based on his life was released. It starred Burt Lancaster.

Rules are like steamrollers

In 1913 a reporter discovered that, years earlier, Thorpe had briefly earned $25 a week playing minor-league baseball. The amount of money was tiny, but technically it made Thorpe a **professional** athlete. All Olympic competitors in those days had to be **amateurs**. Thorpe protested that he had not even known about the amateur rule back then. He also pointed out that since his Olympic triumph, he had turned down offers of thousands of dollars for his talents.

It did no good. His medals were taken back and his feats were wiped out of the Olympic record books. "Rules are like steamrollers," Thorpe wrote later. "There is nothing they won't do to flatten the man who stands in their way." Thorpe's own life went rather flat afterwards. After playing baseball and football for a while, he became a drifter. Jim Thorpe died of a heart attack in 1953.

Most ordinary people felt that Thorpe had been treated very harshly. The people of Mauch Chunk, Pennsylvania, where he was buried, changed their small town's name to Jim Thorpe. In 1951, sportswriters voted him the greatest athlete of the first half of the century. In 1943 his supporters began to request the **reinstatement** of his medals and records. It turned out to be a long campaign, but it finally met with success. In 1982 the International Olympic Committee lifted the ban on Jim Thorpe. His name was written back into the Olympic roll of fame, and in 1983 his gold medals were presented once more to his children.

Racing Against Racism

The International Olympic Committee (IOC) decides where each Olympic Games will be held. It makes its decision several years in advance, so that the host city has plenty of time to prepare. In 1931 the IOC decided that the 1936 Games would be held in Berlin, the capital of Germany. The Germans were one of the world's leading sporting nations, and they could be relied on to organize a successful Olympics. But then in 1933, something unforeseen happened. A new political party was elected to power in Germany. Its name was the National Socialist German Workers' Party—**Nazi** for short—and its leader was Adolf Hitler.

Olympic spirit or Olympic spite?

Soon people inside and beyond Germany learned that Hitler and his followers held racist views. These included the belief that white-skinned, racially pure Germans were superior in all ways to other people, particularly Jews and blacks. Laws were soon passed that discriminated against Jews and other minorities. It became clear that Hitler wanted to use the Berlin Games of August 1936 as a showcase for his idea of the German Master Race.

Jewish communities outside Germany called for a **boycott** of the Games. In the United States there was an especially strong campaign. But the Nazis assured the IOC that they would abide by the rules of Olympic competition. Two "half-Jews" were selected for the German national team. So the Games went ahead as planned.

This is an official poster for the 1936 Olympics.

GERMANY
BERLIN·1936
1ST-16TH AUGUST

OLYMPIC GAMES

Triumph of the black athletes

Before 1936 Germany had not excelled in **track and field** events. But early in the Berlin Games, policeman Hans Woellke became the first German track and field gold medalist ever by winning the shot put. Hitler and his supporters were delighted, but their joy did not last.

Four years after Jesse Owens' death in 1980, a Berlin street was renamed after him. It was a fitting tribute to one of the greatest Olympians of all time.

The United States ended up with 25 medals in track and field. Thirteen were won by African Americans, whom the Nazis called "black **mercenaries**." One of these supreme black athletes was Jesse Owens, gold medalist in the 100-meter run, 200-meter run, long jump, and 4×100-meter relay. In spite of all the Nazi **propaganda**, the German people made Owens the hero of the Games. They even thrust autograph books through his Olympic Village bedroom window while he was trying to sleep!

There is a story that after Owens won the 100-meter run final, a furious Hitler refused to meet him, even though he had congratulated other gold medalists. This may or may not be true. What is true is that when Owens went home to the United States, President Franklin D. Roosevelt failed to invite him to the White House. He did not even send a letter of praise for his awesome Olympic feats. Thanks to racial laws in the United States, Owens, like other black people, was not seen as equal to white Americans. His Olympic brilliance gave a huge boost to the pride of African Americans. But 32 years later, long after Hitler and his hateful ideas had gone, true racial equality had still not been achieved in the Unites States. Once again, racial issues took center stage at the Olympics.

Podium Protests

The 1968 Games in Mexico City were controversial even before they began. The Olympics had never been held at such **altitude** before, more than 6,500 feet (2,000 meters) above sea level. Many experts feared that athletes unused to the very thin air might die from pushing themselves too hard. These were also the Games in which sex tests were introduced, because some women were suspected of chemically improving their bodies with human growth hormones, thus technically making themselves men.

Then, ten days before the Games were to begin, Mexico City became the scene of a bloodbath when the Mexican army opened fire on a student **demonstration**. About 260 people were killed and 1,200 injured. Shock waves from this were felt all around the sporting world. But the International Olympic Committee called it an internal affair, which was under control. The Games could still go on under the official slogan of "Everything is possible with peace."

American or Negro?

Once the Games began, the biggest debate came after the 200-meter run finals for men. African American Tommie Smith cruised home in a new world record time of 19.83 seconds. In third place was fellow African American John Carlos, the previous world record holder. Both men belonged to the Olympic Project for Human Rights, a group of athletes who campaigned for better treatment for blacks in the United States. They wanted the world to know about U.S. racial inequality.

Tommie Smith and John Carlos make their peaceful protest on the podium in Mexico City, 1968. When Carlos was accused of tainting the Games by making a political point, he said the Olympics were already highly political. "Why do they play national anthems?" he asked. "Why can't everyone wear the same colors, but wear numbers to tell them apart? What happened to the Olympic ideal of man against man?"

When Smith and Carlos stepped onto the podium to collect their medals, they were barefoot. And when the U.S. national anthem played, they bowed their heads and raised black-gloved hands in a Black Power salute.

The two men explained later that their bare feet were a reminder of African American poverty, and their clenched fists showed black strength and unity. "White America will only give us credit for an Olympic victory," said Carlos. "They'll say I'm an American, but if I did something bad, they'd say I was a Negro." The U.S. Olympic Committee apparently did not feel the same. Both men were quickly banned from the team and ordered out of the Olympic Village. Back at home, they found it hard to make a living for many years. But they had drawn the world's attention to a very big problem in a completely peaceful way.

Flashback to 1936

At the Berlin Games of 1936 the marathon was won in style by Korean athlete Sohn Kee-Chung. Fellow Korean Nam Seung-Yang picked up the bronze. But at that time their homeland was being **occupied** by Japan, so they were forced to run in the colors of Japan. They even had to take Japanese names. After receiving their medals, they showed their dissatisfaction by bowing their heads in silent protest while the Japanese national anthem was played.

In later years Sohn was able to enjoy the Games a little more. At the opening ceremony in 1948, he carried the flag of a free South Korea. And in 1988 in Seoul, South Korea, Sohn, at the age of 76, carried the Olympic torch into the stadium.

The United States' gold-medal-winning 4 × 400-meter team leaves the arena in Mexico City with a clenched-fist salute to show their support for fellow African Americans.

Black September

The 1972 Games were held in Munich, West Germany. No expense was spared in staging the biggest Olympics ever. The last time the Games had taken place on German soil was in 1936. At that time, Adolf Hitler's ruling **Nazi** Party had tried to undermine the true Olympic spirit. There was to be none of that in 1972, at least not from the organizers. Just before the opening, to make sure that 27 African nations did not carry out their threat to **boycott** the Games, the International Olympic Committee (IOC) expelled Rhodesia (now called Zimbabwe) for its policy of **white supremacy**.

It now seemed that little could go wrong. In purely sporting terms, very little did. With over 4,000 representatives of the world's **media** watching, records tumbled as never before. But the Games' sheer size, and the interest they created all over the world, also attracted to Munich people with no interest in sports. On the morning of September 5, these people made their presence felt.

On September 6, 1972, 84,000 people filled the Olympic stadium in Munich to remember those who had died in the Olympic Games' worst act of terrorism.

Worst-case scenario

The Munich Games were meant to be very friendly. As a result, security was minimal. That was how eight Palestinian Arab **terrorists** managed to get into the Olympic Village. Ever since 1948, Arabs and Israelis had been in conflict with each other in the Middle East. On September 5, 1972, the Arab terrorists headed for the Israeli quarters. They killed two people and took nine **hostages**.

The terrorists demanded the release of 200 Arab prisoners from Israeli jails, as well as a safe passage to Egypt for themselves. After long negotiations, the terrorists and their hostages were allowed to go to the military airport. There, West German marksmen killed three of the terrorists. But a gun battle followed, in which all nine Israeli hostages were killed, along with two more Arabs and a policeman. After such an awful tragedy what could happen next?

The Games must go on

The next morning, the Games were suspended for a memorial service in a packed Olympic stadium. Some people felt that the Games should now be declared over, and a few athletes did leave Munich for fear of another terrorist attack. But finally the IOC decided to continue the program.

The aim of the terrorists had been to disrupt the Games, argued IOC President Avery Brundage, so why should they get what they wanted? Besides, if they managed to stop the Olympics in its tracks, how many other similar groups might try to do the same in future? The Israeli officials were in full agreement with this. The Games went on. And since that dreadful day in 1972, terrorism has not been a major Olympic issue, but providing tight security has been.

The 1972 Games continued, but there were other, lesser controversies. Despite his lunge for the line in the 800-meter run finals, Russian Evgeni Arzhanov lost to Dave Wottle of the United States (shown wearing the hat) by 0.03 seconds. Wottle was so surprised to win that he forgot to remove his hat during the national anthem. People thought he was making a political protest.

Misery in Montreal

Sporting achievements took most of the headlines at the 1976 Games in Montreal, Canada, but in financial terms they could hardly have been more disastrous. For a variety of reasons, the cost of staging the Olympics in 1976 was 60 percent higher than the cost of staging them in Munich four years earlier. When the Games finished, the taxpayers of Montreal had to pay off a **deficit** of $1 billion. It took them until 1996, just before the Atlanta Games, to do this.

Rugby prompts a boycott

Once the Games got under way, there were about 1,000 fewer competitors than there had been in Munich. This was because more than 30 countries were either banned or refused to take part. As in 1972, Rhodesia was banned because blacks and whites were still kept separate due to that country's system of **white supremacy**. The island of Taiwan withdrew because the Canadian Government refused to recognize it as the Republic of China. This name was disputed by mainland, **communist**, China. But by far the largest number of absentee nations were African nations. Their reason for staying away was tied to rugby, which was not even an Olympic sport.

When the 1976 Games opened in Montreal, work on the Olympic facilities was still going on. This was due partly to bad weather conditions during the long winter, partly to workers' strikes, and partly to a serious lack of funds. But the *Montreal Star* newspaper pointed out that the organizers made some strange decisions.

For example, 33 cranes were rented by the builders of the Olympic stadium at a cost of $1 million. Some of the cranes were never used. It would have been cheaper to have bought the cranes outright. Also, because of the terrorist attack at the 1972 Munich Games, officials organized a tighter security operation. This also contributed to the great expense.

The New Zealand rugby team is called the All Blacks (after the color of their outfits). These All Blacks had recently made a tour of South Africa, which, like Rhodesia, was banned from the Olympics because of its **apartheid** policy. Over 20 African nations, plus Guyana and Iraq, demanded that the International Olympic Committee (IOC) should ban New Zealand from the 1976 Olympics. When the IOC refused, the protesting nations, led by Tanzania, took their own action by **boycotting** the Games.

Burning of the boat

In spite of all these troubles, the Montreal Olympics were still hugely enjoyable to watch and to take part in. Triple-gold medalist Nadia Comaneci, a fourteen-year-old Romanian gymnast, became a popular symbol of all that was right about the Games. Even so, not everyone was happy. Two British yachtsmen, Allen Warren and David Hunt, finished fourteenth out of sixteen entries in the Tempest class. After the final race, they calmly set their boat on fire, then waded ashore to watch it burn. "I tried to persuade my skipper [Warren] to burn with the ship," joked Hunt, "but he wouldn't agree."

This is the official poster for the 1976 Games in Montreal, which have gone down in Olympic history as a financial fiasco.

CANADA 1976

The last disappointment came for the poor Canadians themselves. The final medal table showed not a single gold for the host country. This was the first time that had ever happened at the Summer Games.

Medal Muddle

Article 46 of the Olympic rules clearly states that "the Olympic Games are not competitions between nations." It has not always seemed that way. Until 1908 athletes entered the Games as individuals, not as chosen members of a national team. That was the original Olympic ideal. Since then, however, one of the most popular features of any Games has been the medals table.

NATIONAL MEDAL TOTALS, 1928 AND 1976

Amsterdam 1928

	G	S	B
United States	22	18	16
Germany	10	7	14
Finland	8	8	9
Sweden	7	6	12
Italy	7	5	7
Switzerland	7	4	4
France	6	10	5
Netherlands	6	9	4
Hungary	4	5	0
Canada	4	4	7

Montreal 1976

	G	S	B
USSR	49	41	35
East Germany	40	25	25
United States	34	35	25
West Germany	10	12	17
Japan	9	6	10
Poland	7	6	13
Bulgaria	6	9	7
Cuba	6	4	3
Romania	4	9	14
Hungary	4	5	13

G=gold; S=silver; B=bronze

A nation's position in the medals table is determined by its gold medal count, or silver and bronze if it has no gold medals.

The International Olympic Committee does not officially recognize national medal totals. But for the **media** and the public, they are often too fascinating to ignore.

Who are the champions?

The table shows the final medals totals for the 1928 Games in Amsterdam and for the 1976 Games in Montreal. In 1928 all the leading nations came from Europe and North America. By 1976 that had changed, with Cuba, Japan, and the part-Asiatic **USSR** making appearances.

In that year, all top ten nations were under **communist** rule except for the United States, West Germany, and Japan. Throughout the **Cold War** period, many communist governments heavily sponsored sports and then reaped their rewards in Olympic gold medals.

Valeri Borzov of the USSR wins the 200-meter run gold medal at the 1972 Games. He refused to give an interview after the race because, he said, U.S. journalists had insulted him after he won the 100-meter final.

According to one East German official at Montreal in 1976, medal-winning "proved the success of our socialist (communist) system and our training methods." In Western countries such as the United States and West Germany, governments did not usually get so directly involved, but were just as anxious to see their athletes do well. In a way, the struggle to win gold became a kind of sporting warfare.

Basketball battle

Some athletes were dismayed by this international rivalry. Especially upsetting was the rivalry between the United States and the USSR. Montreal champion swimmer John Naber said, "Gold medals don't mean the White House is better than the **Kremlin**. It means I swam faster than anyone else, that's all." But few doubted that more than mere sport was at stake in Munich in 1972 when the United States took on the USSR in the final basketball game.

Ever since 1936, when basketball was first played at the Games, the United States had never lost. And when the horn sounded for the end of this game, the U.S. team was ahead—50 points to 49. But the Brazilian referee overruled the clock. The game was briefly restarted, then the horn sounded again. Now a higher official ruled that, due to an earlier mix up, three more seconds should be added on. The USSR team pulled off a court-long move that ended with a basket. Amid enormous uproar, they were given the victory—51 to 50. The U.S. team, disgusted at having been "cheated," refused to accept their silver medals. To lose any Olympic match was bad enough, but to lose to the USSR in such controversial circumstances was almost unbearable.

The United States had never lost a basketball match at the Olympics before 1972. In 1988, they had to settle for the third-place bronze medal as two communist nations, the USSR and Yugoslavia, played each other in the finals.

Politics Stopped Play

"In ancient days," former International Olympic Committee (IOC) President Avery Brundage once said, "nations stopped wars to compete in the Games. Nowadays we stop the Olympics to continue our wars." Political conflict certainly had an impact on the Games in 1980.

Near misses

David Wallechinsky describes in his book titled *Complete Book of the Olympics* how the various **boycotts** of the 1970s and 1980s affected one unlucky individual. Bruce Kennedy was an excellent javelin thrower from Rhodesia. In 1972, he was selected for the Rhodesian team to travel to Munich. But the IOC banned Rhodesia from taking part because of the racist system of government in that country.

He was selected again for Montreal in 1976, but Rhodesia was still excluded. Then, by marrying an American citizen, he qualified for the U.S. team that would go to Moscow in 1980. That team, of course, never arrived in the **USSR** due to the U.S. boycott of the Games. By then, though, Rhodesia (renamed Zimbabwe) had been allowed back into the Olympics.

In 1984 Kennedy was absolutely determined to get into an Olympic stadium. At last he managed it, as an usher!

U.S. President Jimmy Carter was the man behind the boycott of the 1980 Games in Moscow.

No go for Moscow

Political rivalry between the United States and the USSR had figured in most of the Games since 1952. It came to a head at the 1980 Olympics and threatened to wreck the Olympic Movement. These Games were to be held in Moscow, the capital city of the **communist**-ruled USSR (also known as the Soviet Union). In 1979, Soviet forces invaded Afghanistan, and U.S. President Jimmy Carter responded with a call to boycott the 1980 Games. As a result, a great controversy broke out.

One member of the IOC said it was "unjust to make athletes the conscience of the world." Each National Olympic Committee had to decide what to do. Rule 26 of the Olympic Charter says that the Committees "must be **autonomous** and must resist all pressure of any kind whatsoever, whether of a political, religious, or economic nature." Some governments friendly to the United States, such as Britain and Australia, backed the boycott, but said their athletes could choose for themselves whether or not to travel to Moscow. It was not quite so easy for American athletes. President Carter threatened to **revoke** the passport of any competitor who tried to go to the USSR.

In 1980 Alan Wells (left) became only the second Briton to win the 100-meter run at the Olympic Games. U.S. athletes, who were absent from Moscow, had won twelve of the previous eighteen contests.

In the end only 80 nations took part in the Moscow Games. But more world records were set than in 1976, and there were many memorable contests. But many fans believed the Games were devalued by the absence of the United States, West Germany, China, Japan, and many other great sporting nations in this, the biggest Olympic boycott ever.

The Russians Aren't Coming—but Zola Budd Is!

After the American-led **boycott** of the 1980 Games in the **USSR**, it was the United State's turn to hold the 1984 Games. And guess what? The USSR organized its own fourteen-nation boycott! The Soviet authorities refused to let their athletes attend partly as a protest over **commercialization** and partly due to doubts about the level of security in Los Angeles. It seemed clear to many, however, that this was a simple act of revenge for the 1980 boycott.

Collision course

A new event was due to appear in the **track and field** program at Los Angeles—the 3,000-meter run for women. Two runners with very different backgrounds were determined to take part: Mary Decker of the United States and Zola Budd of South Africa. Decker had been a child **prodigy**. At the age of twelve, she ran a marathon in just over three hours, a 440-meter run, an 880-meter run, a mile race, and a two-mile race—all in the space of one week! Around the age of fifteen, all the running badly affected her growing body, and she missed the 1976 Games due to illness. By 1980, however, she was back with a vengeance, setting a world record for the mile and raring to take on the world's best in the Moscow Games of 1980. The boycott shattered that dream, but also made her more determined to run in her home town of Los Angeles in 1984.

British **decathlon** gold medalist Daley Thompson models an interesting t-shirt in Los Angeles. The back of the shirt criticized the broadcasts of the ABC television network, which focused closely on American winners and not on those of other nations.

ABC paid $225 million for exclusive TV broadcast rights. This was a massive increase from the $394,000 fee paid by CBS in 1960. In the eyes of many people, this led to an unacceptable commercialization of the Games.

Zola Budd's home town was Bloemfontein, South Africa. She had a poster of her hero, Mary Decker, on her bedroom wall. By 1983, at age seventeen and running barefoot, she was ranked number one in the world for the 5,000-meter run. In January 1984, she broke Decker's world record for that distance by six seconds. But to get to Los Angeles, Budd had to change her nationality. As a South African, she was barred from competing. So she moved to Britain, her grandfather's homeland, became a British citizen, and got on the British team.

Decker on the deck

The stage was set for a great Decker–Budd showdown in Los Angeles. It turned out to be one of the most controversial races ever. After 1,700 meters Budd led, followed closely by Decker. What happened next depended on whose side you took. Budd and Decker got into a tangle, and Budd was briefly thrown off balance. Five strides later, it happened again. Decker tripped over Budd's leg, cutting the barefoot leader's heel with her spikes. Decker fell awkwardly and was out of the race in agony.

Budd (151) vs. Decker (373) was one of many events in 1984 that was scheduled so it could be broadcast during prime time in the U.S., even though it was the middle of the night in Europe.

Budd ran on, bleeding from the clash, and soon crying, too, because Decker's home crowd of over 85,000 was booing her loudly. She came in seventh and was disqualified for causing Decker's downfall. Later, that decision was overruled, but a huge dispute played out in the U.S. and British **media** over who had been at fault. In the end, almost everyone agreed that it had been an unfortunate accident. Neither woman was destined to ever win a medal at any future Games.

Failing the Test

For many people, the men's 100-meter sprint is the biggest Olympic event. As the athletes lined up for the 100-meter finals in Seoul in 1988, the world held its breath. In under ten seconds, the World's Fastest Man would be revealed. Carl Lewis, the 1984 champion, was running. So was world record holder Ben Johnson from Canada. Lewis suspected that Johnson took illegal drugs called steroids to improve his performance. Just 9.79 seconds later, Johnson thrust his arm in the air to smash his own world record. Second-place Lewis was surer than ever that Johnson had cheated, and at the post-race drug test, he was proven right.

"I know what it's like to cheat."

Drug testing of urine samples was introduced at the 1968 Olympics. Since then 42 athletes had been disqualified and disgraced for failing their tests. Ben Johnson was the 43rd, but no one this famous had ever been caught.

Passing the test

At the 1968 Games in Mexico, British bricklayer Chris Finnegan won the middleweight boxing crown. He could barely describe his feelings. "The nearest I've felt to it was walking down the aisle after our wedding, only there was no gold medal at the end of that!" But then he had to perform again by giving a urine sample for drug testing. To everyone's frustration, it took him until 1:40 the next morning before he could provide the sample. He passed the test.

Ben Johnson of Canada won the Seoul 100-meter final in 1988 by a margin that was just too big to be true.

Shock waves from Seoul rippled all over the world, and then it got worse. Later inquiries showed that Johnson had been taking steroids since 1981, plus growth hormones taken from human corpses. In 1989 Johnson publicly confessed and pleaded with young athletes not to follow his example. "It happened to me," he said in tears. "I've been there. I know what it's like to cheat."

Supersprinter Florence Griffith-Joyner of the United States won three gold medals at Seoul, South Korea. Some people suspected "Flojo" of using drugs to achieve phenomenal racing times after an unspectacular start to her career. She passed every drug test she took, but retired in 1989 just before random (unannounced) testing began.

Sadly, she died of a heart seizure in 1998, at the age of 38. People who still suspected her pointed out that steroid use can lead, in the long term, to an overloading of the heart and damage to the **arteries**. One of the sad effects of drug-taking in sports is that any amazing feat immediately seems suspicious, even if the athlete is completely innocent.

All in the blood

Steroids are not the only way athletes can enhance their performance. There is a technique called blood doping, now illegal, which involves taking out some of an athlete's blood, storing it for a week or two, then re-injecting it just before a big race. This improves the body's intake of oxygen.

Some people suspected Lasse Viren, the Finnish distance runner who won two gold medals at both the 1972 and 1976 Games, of blood doping. Nothing was ever proven, and Viren always laughed at the suspicions, saying that he trained "on reindeer milk." But in 1984, another Finn, Martti Vainio, lost his 10,000-meter run silver medal when traces of a steroid were found in his sample. It is believed that he stopped taking steroids three weeks before the race, hoping not to be caught. But because of blood doping, steroids were put back into his bloodstream.

From Atlanta to Australia

Terrorist attacks have been mercifully rare at the modern Olympic Games. Since the tragedy at Munich in 1972, each host city has made security a top priority. But at the **Centennial** Games in Atlanta in 1996, terrorism reared its grotesque head again.

On Day Nine of the Games, a crude pipe bomb exploded inside the Centennial Olympic Park. This was a 22-acre (9-hectare) area of corporate tents where sports fans from all over the world could meet and enjoy the Olympic atmosphere. The bomb killed two people and wounded about 100 others.

Atlanta had advertised itself as "a city too busy to hate." Clearly, that was not absolutely true. But, three days after the bombing, the park reopened and the fans flocked back. Like the Munich Games in 1972, the show had to go on, in spite of this sick and cowardly attempt to disrupt it.

In recent years, the high cost of staging the Games has led to more involvement by large corporations. The Coca-Cola Company, headquartered in Atlanta, Georgia, was closely involved in the bidding for the 1996 Olympics.

The Company finally spent about $200 million on its Olympic sponsorship, including advertising. This led some to refer to the 1996 Olympics as the "Coke Games." As one International Olympic Committee vice-president put it, "No matter where the Games are, Coca-Cola will be there."

Many people are upset by this sort of **commercialization**. They feel that the Games are turning from a friendly athletic competition into just another big business.

On to Sydney, 2000

The Games in the year 2000 will be held in Sydney, Australia. The last time Australia staged the Games was in 1956, and Melbourne was host city. That was in the middle of the **Cold War**. The Netherlands, Switzerland, and Spain **boycotted** the Games in a protest against the **USSR's** brutal treatment of Hungarians following a political uprising in Hungary. Egypt, Lebanon, and Iraq also withdrew in protest at the Israeli-led takeover of the Suez Canal. Further difficulties were caused by Australia's location. In 1956 it was difficult and expensive for many of the world's best athletes to travel to Australia.

Getting to Sydney in 2000 should not be too great a problem. More than 10,000 competitors and a million spectators from overseas are expected to take part. What they will witness at the Millennium Games cannot be predicted. But if previous Games are anything to go by, there will almost certainly be some kind of controversy.

Just as in earlier Games held in the United States, there were murmurings of discontent in Atlanta about local favoritism.

The American runner Michael Johnson wanted to become the first man in history to win both the 200-meter and the 400-meter run. But the scheduling of track events made it impossible for him to make the attempt. Amid some controversy, the organizers decided to alter the program to let Johnson take part in both events.

In due course this extraordinary athlete won two gold medals and set a phenomenally fast, new world record time of 19.32 seconds in the 200-meter run.

29

Glossary

altitude height above sea level

amateur someone who competes for fun, rather than as a job, and who is unpaid

apartheid former South African political policy of keeping black people apart from white people

artery blood vessel that carries blood away from the heart

autonomous self-governing, free from outside interference

boycott to refuse to have anything to do with a person, country, or event

bust sculpture of a person's head, shoulders, and chest

centennial the hundredth anniversary

Cold War period after World War II of unfriendly relations (yet no actual warfare) between the United States and the USSR

commercialization attempt to make money from something

communism political, economic, and social system that has state-owned land, factories, and means of production. After World War II, the USSR introduced communism into much of eastern Europe.

consolation a prize given not for winning, but for being a runner-up

decathlon competition consisting of ten different track and field events: 100-meter run, 110-meter hurdles, 400-meter run, 1,500-meter run, high jump, long jump, pole vault, javelin throw, discus throw, and shot put

deficit amount by which a sum of money is too small. For example, if someone needs $5 and has only $1, there is a deficit of $4.

demonstration public protest about an issue

hostage someone who is held as a prisoner until certain demands are met

intercollegiate competition between different colleges

interim taking place between official Games

Kremlin headquarters of the government of the USSR

media plural of medium (of communication), for example newspapers, magazines, TV, and radio

mercenary person who is purely working for pay or other rewards

Nazi member or supporter of the National Socialist German Workers' Party, a political party led by Adolf Hitler

occupied invaded and held by force

pentathlon athletic contest in which a competitor takes part in five different track and field events

prodigy someone, especially a child, who is very talented

professional paid competitor

propaganda information meant to convince people of an idea or view

reinstatement restoration

revoke take away

royal box special seats from which a royal family views public events

terrorist someone who uses violence to force a government to do what he or she wants

track and field sporting events which involve running, jumping, throwing, and walking

USSR communist country which included Russia and other nations. It divided into separate nations in 1991.

white supremacy political arrangement or system of government by which white people, although small in numbers, have more rights and privileges than the black majority

More Books to Read

Anderson, Dave. *The Story of the Olympics*. New York: William Morrow & Company, 1996.

Hunter, Shawn. *Great African Americans in the Olympics*. New York: Crabtree Publishing Company, 1997.

Italia, Robert. *100 Unforgettable Moments in the Summer Olympics*. Minneapolis: ABDO Publishing Company, 1996.

Index